The Complete Book of Wicker & Cane Furniture Making

The Complete Book of
Wicker
&
Cane
Furniture
Making

by

John Bausert

Drake Publishers Inc.
New York · London

Published in 1976 by
Drake Publishers, Inc.
801 Second Avenue
New York, N.Y. 10017

© Copyright in 1976 by John Bausert

Design and Calligraphy by Eleanor Winters

Library of Congress Cataloging in Publication Data
Bausert, John.
    The complete book of wicker and cane furniture making.

    1. Wicker furniture.   I. Title.   II. Title:
Cane furniture.
TT197.7.B38   684.1'06   75-36148
ISBN 0-8473-1064-7
ISBN 0-8473-1182-1 pbk.

Printed in the United States of America

DEDICATION

To my father — who never pushed.

ACKNOWLEDGEMENTS

I would like to thank the following people for their invaluable help and knowledge. My wife Susan, my father, my brother Warren, John LeMaire, Mary Ann Eckels, Simon Eckels, Vivian Alford, and Sumner Bryant of Commonwealth Manufacturing, who helped with the origins of caning.

Finally, I would like to thank my wonderful three year old son, Sean; thank him for the time that I should have been playing with him.

Contents

Preface

This volume provides both the novice and skilled craftsperson with a guide for making handcrafted furniture and decorative objects. The specific projects described and illustrated in the text have been selected for their simplicity of construction and pleasing design. Once the projects are completed, the development of each skill will enable the individual to translate this knowledge to more complex projects of his own choosing and design concept. All of the projects described herein can be completed using simple tools and equipment found in most home workshops and the supplies to be purchased are nominal in cost.

Thus, the intention is to provide a fundamental explanation of technique as well as a comprehensive knowledge of the origin, history and various uses of the materials. Those examined are handcaning, prewoven or machine caning, fiber rush, splint and wickerwork. With the exception of wickerwork, each of the other four techniques describes repair and restoration procedures. The wicker section includes the actual construction as well. Illustrations and photographs by the author accompany each chapter and provide visual data and an overall pictorial view of these special handcrafts. Along with the obvious achievement of creating functional and aesthetically pleasurable objects, the joy of making something by hand is most rewarding.

Introduction

For centuries, objects and products of natural rattan materials have been enjoyed as furniture and functional items as well as decoration and art. While rattan is one of mankind's earliest known materials, and the methods of production have remained essentially the same, advanced technology and design concept have facilitated its use in many aspects of modern life. Anthropological recognition of these materials can be traced to the earliest evidence of civilization in China and Egypt. By contrast, they can be observed today in modern home furnishings and the fashion industry to coincide with the trend back to the use of natural products and handcrafts. The very nature of the material provides flexibility and endurance. Currently, the renewal of interest in the use of natural materials, including cane and rattan, has led to incorporation of these materials with natural woods, chrome or other metals, and plastic and plexiglass. Also, a revival of interest in period antiques requires these materials and skills for restoration or repair.

A method of mass production, certainly a unique one, was employed in an account of Chinese history describing how rattan was woven through knives tied to oxen which were then forced to run in carefully calculated directions to produce woven chair cane. Today's method is simpler — woven chair cane is produced on looms in great quantity at less cost and effort. In the late nineteenth century, Cyrus Wakefield conceived and perfected the machinery to cut cane material. At approximately the same time, Gardiner A. Watkins invented the spline and groove machine method of chair caning and also developed the equipment to weave machine cane material.

Hand caning became popular initially in this country in the 1700s when the cost of doing a hand-caned chair was approximately fifteen cents. The use of these materials continued into the nineteenth century and they were used extensively in early American furniture construction. In the late 1920s, paper products were first introduced for cane webbing as were the newly invented synthetics and plastics. During World War II, a government embargo restricted the importation of caning materials from the Far East and South Pacific areas, the main supply sources. Prior to the popularity of synthetic materials in this country, cane webbing had a variety of uses including its incorporation into the inner lining of army caps to maintain shape and give proper ventilation.

Rattan is a climbing palm with very long, tough stems. Cane is made from rattan. Rattan is found in all parts of the world; however, only certain types of rattan are usable for caning and wickerwork and these are mostly imported from Indonesia, Malaysia and Sumatra at the present time. Rattan grows in dense, tropical jungle areas where it is considered a secondary forest product. There are as many as two hundred different types which are all included in the palm family. The plant itself grows upward and downward in an undulating manner, due to its weight, until it attaches to a tree branch, at which time it will continue to grow climbing along the tree tops. Rattan is not related to bamboo although they are often confused; the former is a solid growth, the latter is hollow. The length of growth of rattan can vary from three feet to more than 400 or 500 feet, although the best quality cane rattan is considered to be between 150 and 200 feet in its natural state. The usable rattan has a diameter of 1/8 inch up to 3-1/4 inches although the larger diameter rattan is unusual.

Rattan reaches maturity when it is the desired length and diameter and has a characteristically thorny bark. The initial stage of harvesting mature rattan, which grows rapidly, involves cutting the rattan vines about three feet from the ground level enabling the vine to regenerate new growth. Once this process is completed, the cut stock is allowed to remain untouched until the bark and thorns have either fallen off or become soft and easily removed. The vines are then pulled from the tree tops and are cut on the ground into usable 16 to 25 foot lengths. These pieces are bundled and the outside hard surface material is removed leaving the remaining soft inside layer exposed.

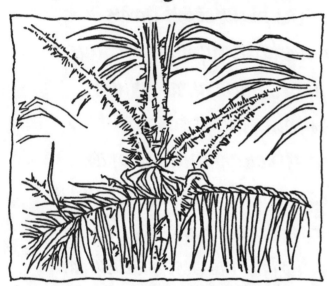 

Once at the storage warehouse, the rattan is washed and treated with sulfur to destroy insects and determine uniformity of color by bringing out natural color highlights. The rattan is then placed in a water bath to remove surface dirt and debris and soften the fiber. Collected and processed rattan is then taken to a plant or cane cutting facility, where it is graded for size in 1/2 to one millimeter increments. The next step involves the scraping or shaving of

the knots or joints where the leaves were attached to the vine.
Once this is completed, the rattan is placed in a roller
machine which peels off the outer surface. This process
yields a hard outer shell which is natural chair cane. This
peeled material is then passed through a slicing machine
which cuts the cane into a specified uniform thickness and
width. Cane webbing or prewoven machine cane is made
from such chair cane. The long strips of cane are glued
end to end, wound on a spool, and woven on looms into
the desired patterns. Other products of the same process
include the center core of the rattan used as spline for
machine caning and also used for wickerwork. Most
splint comes from split rattan and fiber rush is a paper
product. All of these materials and their uses will be
fully documented on the following pages.

Chapter 1
Hand Caning

Hand caning is a weaving process whereby each step locks the previous one in place, which ultimately creates a sturdy, flexible surface of natural fibers. The method described is most frequently used by professionals in the industry, as well as by skilled craftsmen. It is known to be the most efficient and expedient. At the present time, hand caning is used predominantly in the restoration of antique furniture, artifacts and for reproductions of period furniture. Its utilization in modern products is restricted, however, due to increased labor costs, making hand caning economically unfeasible for production in quantity.

This chapter describes and illustrates in detail the seven step weaving method. Also included are the tools and materials, selection and preparation of cane, and final finishing of a hand-caned chair seat. Once this weaving technique is mastered, it can be applied to any hand caning project.

TOOLS and MATERIALS

In addition to the chair seat frame to be hand-caned

17

and the actual cane material, the following tools are required.

1. Hammer
2. Awl or ice pick
3. Utility knife (Stanley makes a very good one)
4. Wooden pegs, either whittled down from soft wood or purchased already made
5. Bowl or pail for water in which to soak cane
6. Rag or cloth used to dampen cane while in use
7. Candle — preferably white in color — used to wax the underside of the cane for ease in weaving

SELECTION of CANE

The determination is made on the basis of the diameter or size of the holes in the chair seat frame and the distance between the holes in the rails:

Size of Cane	Diameter of Holes	Distance between Holes
Carriage cane	1/8 inch or less	3/8 inch or less
Superfine	1/8 inch	3/8 inch
Fine fine	3/16 inch	1/2 inch
Fine	3/16 to 1/4 inch	5/8 inch

Size of Cane	Diameter of Holes	Distance between Holes
Medium	1/4 inch	3/4 inch
Common	5/16 inch	7/8 inch

The best quality cane is glossy in appearance and smooth in texture on one side. It should be tough and pliable, resisting a tendancy to break or split. The knots and joints where the leaves were attached to the stalk should be unbroken and shaved smooth.

Normally, cane can be purchased in chair lots or hanks. Chair lots of caning material are 250 feet in length and hanks of caning material are 1000 feet in length. In addition, a strip of binding cane is provided at the time of purchase. Binding cane is slightly wider and coarser than the type used for the actual weaving of the seat. The length of the binding should approximate one and one half times the perimeter of the chair seat frame.

PREPARATION of CANE

Separate three or four strands of cane from the bundle and soak them in lukewarm water for a period of 10 or 15 minutes. As each strand is used, it should be replaced with another in the water. If the cane is not thoroughly soaked, it is more likely to break during the weaving process and will lack pliability, whereas oversoaking could render the cane limp and weaken the strands. Prior to weaving, it is advisable to lightly pull or rub the strands between the fingers to smooth out the kinks and remove excess water. During the weaving process, the shiny or glossy side of the cane should appear on the top surface, with the dull, rough side on the bottom.

WEAVING

Step #1 The First Vertical Weave

Count the number of holes in both the front and back rails of the chair seat frame to determine which are the center holes. Place a wooden peg in the center hole on both the front and back rails. If the number of holes is even, place the peg in the hole nearest the left side of the chair as you are facing it. The holes with the peg markers should be aligned directly front and rear. Once the center determination has been made, remove the peg on the back rail and insert four to five inches of cane downward into the hole being sure the shiny surface is up. Pull this end through the hole and loop it around the back rail of the chair placing the excess back down the same hole and secure by replacing the peg. Take the opposite end of the cane and pull it across to the front or forward rail and down the hole where the peg has been temporarily removed. Pull it through the hole so that the strand remains taut, but not tight, and

replace the peg. Bring the cane up through the next hole to the left and extend it across to the back rail. Insert it down the hole directly to the left of the previous strand. Secure it with a peg. This same procedure is continued until the strand of cane is completely used.

To end the first piece, bring the cane up the next consecutive hole leaving three to four inches protruding above the rail. Place the new strand of cane down the same hole where the previous strand ended. To knot the new strand, slip it through the loop formed by the piece of cane that was brought up and left on top, on the underside of the chair. At the same time, go back through the loop that is formed by the new piece. This second loop was formed after going

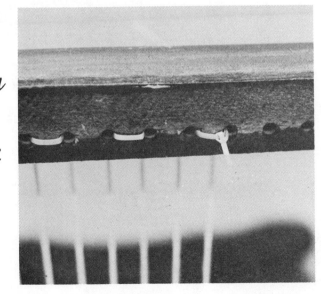

through the first loop. Pull up on the end of the cane protruding on the top side of the chair. The end of the new strand should then be pulled toward the front of the chair. The cane is now secure and the weaving process can continue. Caution should be taken to be certain the cane does not twist or split.

Hand caning the seat of an irregular shaped chair requires some flexibility in weaving. The traditional basic seat shapes are square and rectangular, sometimes wider in front and gradually narrowing in the rear. Variations of these basic shapes are considered irregular and, in hand caning, the primary concern is to insure that all of the lines are parallel. In some cases, once all of the holes are completed on the back rail, some unused ones will remain in the front. When this occurs, the procedure is to weave the cane from the unused holes on the front rail into selected appropriate holes on the side rails. In order to do this, select the hole that will most nearly retain the parallel lines of the woven design. It will be necessary to skip some holes on the side rails to maintain nearly parallel lines overall. This procedure is similar for caning round or oval shaped chair seats.

The first vertical weave, or Step #1, is completed when the back and forward movement uses all of the parallel holes with the exception of the holes in each of the four corners. These will be utilized in later steps of the weaving process.

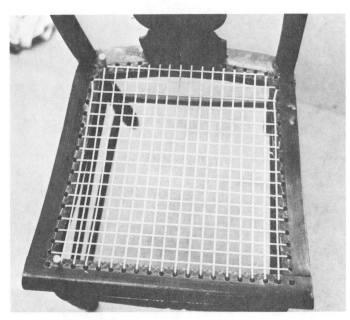

Step #2 The First Horizontal Weave

Repeat the same process as described in Step #1 using the left and right side rails of the chair seat. The horizontal parallel strands are woven on top of the vertical ones. Continue the process keeping in mind that all four corner holes will still remain unused.

The chair seat should be dampened with a wet cloth at frequent intervals during the weaving process. This insures that it will remain soft and pliable for working. Both the top and underside of the seat should remain moist but not wet. Be as careful as possible not to get water on the chair finish. If some water does get on the finish, wipe immediately with a dry cloth. This will keep the finish from getting water spots.

Unfortunately, if the strand of cane should split or break, it should be removed and replaced to maintain the structure and durability as well as the appearance of the final product. It is further advisable to utilize the strands of cane at their full length as opposed to short strips which are less durable.

Step #3 The First Diagonal Weave

As you are facing the chair, the first diagonal weave is begun in the right front corner. Insert three to four inches of cane into the first hole on the front rail to the left of the right corner hole. Secure this strand of cane with a peg. The free end of the cane is then woven or "threaded" down the first hole on the right rail next to the corner hole. Pull the strand tight. Come up the next adjoining hole and continue to weave in this diagonal direction. The diagonal weave is always woven over the top of the horizontal lines, Step #2, and under the vertical lines, Step #1. If necessary, the awl or ice pick can be used to lift the strands and is also helpful when inserted into the holes which have already had cane woven into them. The action of placing the awl down the hole will compact the cane leaving room for the additional strands to be woven through the same holes. This tool must be used delicately, however, so as not to split or damage the cane. The diagonal lines, as well as the vertical and horizontal lines, should be kept parallel. In order to maintain this structure, it may be necessary to skip some holes on the left side of the chair as the weaving continues. The number of holes that are doubled on one side of the chair seat during the diagonal weave will be the same number of holes skipped on the opposite side. This can be determined visually and with discretion and good judgment. The weave continues as described until a corner hole is encountered.

All of the corner holes have two diagonal strands woven into them. This will retain the evenness of the lines that were previously woven. Thus, the first half of the diagonal weave will be symmetrical with the second half of the diagonal weave.

In order to determine when to use more than one strand of cane in the same hole, discounting corner holes, the diagonals are doubled when there are more lines than there are holes to accommodate them. This is done to maintain the symmetry of the chair seat and keep the diagonal lines parallel or as nearly parallel as possible.

Again, the seat should be frequently dampened both on the top and bottom sides as the weaving continues.

Step #4 The Second Vertical Weave

This step is woven exactly in line with, and slightly to the right of Step #1. Also, Step #4 is woven on top of the first three steps. Continue weaving until you have as many vertical lines now as you had in Step #1.

Step #5 The Second Horizontal Weave

This is considered both the most difficult and the most rewarding step and will be the most time consuming. Begin at the left back corner of the chair. Careful use of the awl or ice pick is most helpful during this particular weaving step. Use the awl to lift and separate the strands of woven cane. The second horizontal weave should be woven in back of the first horizontal weave as described in Step #2. Before beginning this step, it is advisable to pull the underneath side of the cane across a candle, or candlewax, which will provide some ease in weaving and reduce friction against the previously woven strands of cane. Begin weaving, as illustrated, under the diagonal lines described in Step #3 and under the first vertical weave in Step #1. Subsequently, the weave should progress over the top of the second vertical, or Step #4, which should be pushed slightly to the right of the first vertical weave, Step #1. It is recommended to weave four or five stitches and then pull the entire piece of cane through. If the entire line is woven first and then the strand of cane pulled through, it is likely that the strand of cane will split or break. It is advisable to master this style of weaving on this step, and the final step, as it will alleviate the necessity of replacing the strand of cane once it becomes weak or actually breaks.

The second line of cane to be woven during this step is the one closest to the front rail. This is imperative as it will insure that the second vertical line will "lay over" and out of the way of the first vertical line. Additional pieces of cane are added as before. The balance of the strand of cane that will appear on the underside of the seat as this first

line is woven can remain there to be woven into the design at a later time. Just remember to dampen it before using. The vertical lines should now be separated at both the top and bottom of the chair seat. This will make the weaving of Step # 5 an easier task. Continue weaving until the entire step is completed. Dampen the cane periodically so that the weaving process is made easier.

Step # 6 The Second Diagonal Weave

Prior to beginning this step of weaving, it is suggested that the awl or ice pick be inserted in each of the holes to ascertain that there will be sufficient room to insert this final additional strand effortlessly. It can also be inserted into the holes created by the weaving to obtain a clear and regular pattern. This step progresses in a similar manner as Step # 3, except for the fact that the cane is worked in the opposite direction. Therefore, the initial strand of cane will be placed at the left corner of the seat on the front rail. Start by bringing the strand of cane up through the hole adjacent to the corner hole in the front rail. Weave the cane under the first diagonal and over the top of the second diagonal line going to the corner hole. The progression is then downward into the corresponding hole on the outside rail. At this point, the cane should be waxed as described in Step #5. Without exception, the weave is over the vertical lines and underneath the horizontal lines during this step. To obtain this pattern always weave over the two vertical lines and also, over the top of the first diagonal that was woven. Then weave under the two horizontal lines and the next diagonal. As previously indicated, the strands of cane should be completely pulled through after every four to five stitches to prevent breakage. Further, during this step, as in Step #3, it will be necessary to skip some holes on the side rail. Each individual chair seat will vary with regard to the number of holes skipped to maintain the correct  design. Also, two pieces of cane will be used in some holes to keep the symmetry of the chair. This was discussed in

Step #3. The weaving then continues until this step is completed and the entire surface forms a pattern of weaving resembling similar shaped hexagonal holes with two each of vertical, horizontal and diagonal lines.

Step #7 Binding

Binding the outside edge of the chair seat requires utilization of two types of cane — the type used for weaving and the wider and heavier binding cane. The binding cane will completely cover the holes of the chair seat frame whereas the regular cane will be used to hold the binding cane in place. Soak the binding cane in warm water for ten minutes. Using a razor knife, cut off any loose ends of cane that may be protruding from the holes on the top of the chair.

To start, secure the regular cane in the first hole from the corner hole, as illustrated, and move the strand of cane up one hole and back down the same hole, creating a loop. Place the binding cane in the corner hole and secure it in place with a wooden peg. Insert the free end of binding cane in loop created by weaving cane. Hold the binding cane in place with an awl. Continue to pull the weaving cane down until it wraps around the awl and binding cane. Slip the awl out and snug the weaving cane around the binding cane. The loop should then be tapped flat on top of the binder. This can be accomplished using the back of the awl. Skip the next hole and then repeat the looping and binding step in the following hole. It is not necessary to bind every hole. Continue the process until the entire surface of the chair seat is bound completely.

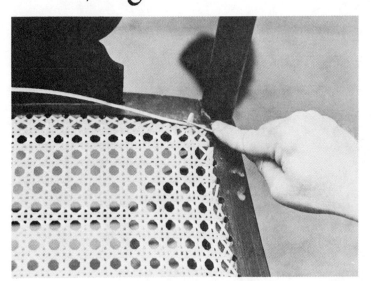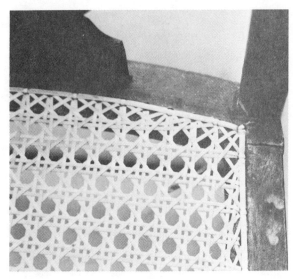

Concluding the binding step requires placing the beginning and ending pieces of binding cane down into the same corner hole that you started with. A sufficient length of binding cane to accomplish this is between 1/4 and 1/2 inch. It should then be fastened with a wooden plug carved or whittled from a small piece of soft wood to fit precisely into the corner hole. The plug can then be hammered into the hole. Make sure that the top of the plug is flush with the wood on the chair seat frame, and smooth to the touch.

The final finishing of the hand-caned chair seat

requires turning the chair upside down to view the underside of the seat which will have a number of loose strands of cane and assorted end pieces. These can now be tied off in the form of the

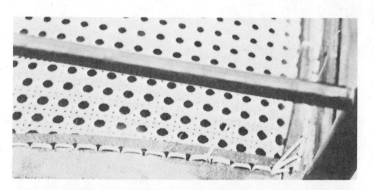

looped knots illustrated. Finally, the top surface should be examined for rough edges or "hairs," which, if they exist, can be carefully removed using a razor knife.

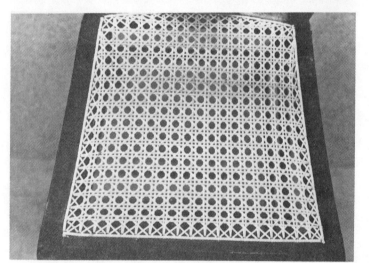

The hand-caned chair seat is now completed. If left in its natural state, the cane will darken in color, developing a patina with age, which is considered desirable. To maintain strength and durability, the cane should be lightly dampened with water once each month and will, with proper care, last for many years. Stain or varnish can be added for color and sheen but this is optional and a matter of personal preference. Interesting detail can be added by stenciling or painting on the cane. This, however, reduces the durability of the cane, as it makes the cane dry and brittle.

Chapter 2

Prewoven or Machine Caning

This type of caning material requires no weaving as in the hand caning process. This cane is prewoven on a loom and can be purchased in the desired length and width. Again, the project selected is the restoration of a chair seat and the steps are described and illustrated. This workmanship can be applied to a variety of furniture styles and decorative pieces. Machine cane is also used in the design and construction of new furniture. It is frequently used on radiator coverings, framed in kitchen cabinet fronts and room dividers. Installation can be effectively accomplished with staples (covered with molding), or with glue and reed spline. This type of cane is also used indoors on yachts because it is lightweight and durable.

Prewoven or machine cane, which is inexpensive and practical, incorporates both the elements of hand craftsmanship and industrial technology and affords flexibility in design and function.

TOOLS and MATERIALS

In addition to the chair to be caned, the actual

caning material and reed spline, the following list of tools is required to do a complete and competent job.

1. Hammer
2. Wood chisel
3. Two hardwood wedges
4. Utility knife
5. Tin snips or large scissors
6. Sandpaper (fine grit)
7. Vinegar (optional)
8. Glue — most any can be used, but a

water-soluble glue is preferred for two reasons. First, if there is a spill, it is very easy to clean, and second, while working with the caning itself, all excess glue wipes off with a damp rag. Note: Hot glue is not recommended because you are working with cold materials and it has a tendancy to damage the cane.

SELECTION of CANE

Prewoven or machine cane comes in two predominant patterns which are standard weave and modern weave. Standard weave is the same design as hand caning with hexagonal shaped holes, whereas modern weave cane comes in either a close weave or open mesh type. Machine cane is woven on looms in 12 to 36 inch widths in two inch increments and is normally supplied in 50 foot rolls. However, varying lengths can be purchased from a retail supplier. The supplier will usually charge by the square foot. The amount required will depend upon the actual size of the chair seat with two additional inches added each way to accommodate the installation. Further, a length of spline is necessary to secure the cane material onto the chair seat frame. The amount can be determined by measuring the circumference or perimeter of the seat. An additional two to four inches of spline will suffice to balance the overlap. Spline is obtained from the inside of the rattan and is either round or wedge shaped. Round spline is most commonly used on chair backs and the wedge shaped variety is used on chair seats. The spline also can be purchased in various lengths and widths and the size selected should be approximately 1/16 of an inch smaller than the groove on the chair seat.

APPLICATION of MACHINE or PREWOVEN CANE
Step #1 Preparation of the Chair Seat

In restoration or repair of the chair seat, the first step is to remove the previously used old cane and clean the groove completely. All of the old spline should be removed with a wood chisel which is slightly smaller than the groove, taking care not to damage the wood surface. If there are any stubborn places where the spline and glue will not come out easily, soaking with vinegar will loosen the old spline and dissolve the remaining glue particles. When the groove is completely free of old cane, spline and glue, carefully sand the area to insure removal of all debris. The most effective way of doing this is to  cut a sheet of sandpaper into four inch by four inch pieces, and fold these into quarter sections. Starting at one front corner, sand back and forth along the inside edge with five or six strokes.

Repeat the same procedure on the outside edge of the same rail, making sure that you do a small area at a time. Continue in the same manner until the entire groove is fully sanded. Then, turn the chair upside down and shake or tap it to force any debris to fall out of the groove.

While this procedure may seem tedious and difficult, it is essential to insure that the replacement cane and spline will adhere properly to the chair seat. This will alleviate the possibility of damaging the cane upon installation and result in a smooth even surface with equal tension in all directions. The additional expenditure of effort in this preliminary step will ultimately prove rewarding. Therefore, patience and care should be exercised during the preparatory stage.

Step #2 Measuring and Cutting the Cane

Cut the machine cane approximately 1/2 inch larger than the outer edge of the groove around the entire seat. If there is more than 1/2 inch overhang, it will prove difficult to work. Next, soak the cane for 10 to 15 minutes

in warm water but never hot water. Remove the cane from the water and allow it to stand for two minutes in order for the excess water to drip off. At this time, the spline is to be placed in the water to soak for approximately 20 minutes. The cane can now be placed on the chair frame and straightened. The horizontal lines of the cane are aligned with the straight edge of the front rail or they are aligned with the joints where the wood is pieced together. For a rounded front rail, align the horizontal lines of cane with the joints of the seat.

Step #3 Attaching the Cane

Using the blunt wood wedge, tap the cane carefully

into the groove, beginning at the center of the back rail and completing a two inch area. Then move to the front of the chair and, before tapping the cane into the groove, straighten the cane and pull it taut. Hold the cane in position on the front rail and tap it into the groove three or four inches to the left and right of the center. Then move to the back rail and attach a few inches more of the cane. Again, move to the front rail and continue the same back and forth movement until the cane is completely attached. Follow the same procedure on the side rails.

Step #4 Application of the Spline

Once all of the cane has been inserted into the groove, run a "bead" of glue into the groove on top of the cane. The amount of glue should remain uniform. Be careful not to be excessive because when tapping the spline down, it will cause the glue to "bubble" up out of the groove and run onto the chair frame. If the seat of the chair is square-shaped, the corners of the spline must be mitred. This will give a neater appearance when the seat is finished. For a round or oval shaped seat, the spline should be cut straight down with a razor knife at a ninety degree angle.

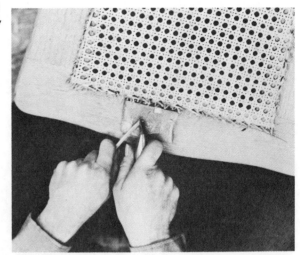

Begin at the left front corner on square chair seats by inserting the spline into the groove and tapping lightly on the spline with the hammer, moving the entire length of the side rail. Repeat this procedure on all sides making certain the mitred joints are neat and clean. Next, tap the spline down with the hammer and

wood wedge that is slightly more blunt than the one used to insert the cane material. When working with a round seat, start at the back rail and tap the spline down with the hammer and wedge for the entire circumference of the seat, working back to the starting point. Then, mark the spline slightly where it will be cut and place the cutting mark on a wood block. Cut it off sharply at the marking by pressing hard using a razor knife. Finally, with a hammer or mallet and wood wedge, pound the spline into the groove making certain it is even overall.

Step # 5 Finishing

The excess cane material is removed from the outer edge of the groove by starting at the right rear of the chair. Hold the cane away from the spline and groove, as illustrated.

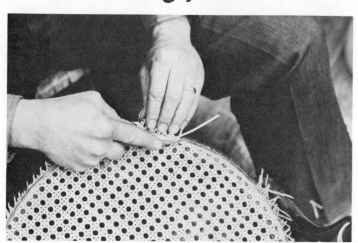

Place the knife blade against the wood frame and draw the knife back along the shape of the groove. It is important to use a very sharp knife blade and exert caution to avoid injury or inadvertently cutting into the cane or the chair. Continue around the entire groove brushing the excess cane away with a damp cloth which will absorb the excess glue. When the excess cane is removed, wipe the groove surface with a warm, damp cloth which will clean off all of the remaining glue particles. As a final step, re-tap the spline to insure that it is completely attached and entirely even.

The chair seat should be allowed to remain untouched for at least 24 hours to make certain it is completely dry. The cane will darken naturally with age if it remains untreated or it can be stained to enhance the appearance. Stain, varnish or paint can be applied as described in the hand caning section. To maintain durability and longevity while resisting stress, the caned chair seat should be dampened with water once each month.

Chapter 3
Fiber Rush

Natural rush is a tufted, reedy marsh plant, sometimes referred to as cattail, with cylindrical, hollow stems and broad leaves that can be used for chair seating or woven mats. The plant leaves are collected and cured or treated to obtain weaving material. Fiber rush is the modern or synthetic adaptation of true natural rush. It is essentially twisted paper formed into a continuous filament. When restoring an antique piece of furniture, it is desirable to use natural rush to maintain authenticity in appearance; however, to repair or restore a less valuable piece, fiber rush, as described in this chapter, is preferable. Fiber rush is more easily woven and less expensive than real or natural rush.

Fiber rush is available in a variety of sizes and several shades of earth tones, predominantly greenish bronze or brownish beige. Fiber rush can be purchased by the pound and 2-1/2 pounds should be sufficient for completion of a chair seat resembling the one described and illustrated here. Further, the basic weaving process used in this chapter can be adapted for use with rope, seagrass or any other suitable cord-like material with equal success. The experienced weaver may also achieve special effects by creating variations on the basic design described here.

TOOLS and MATERIALS

In addition to the chair seat to be woven and the fiber rush, the following tools and materials are required.

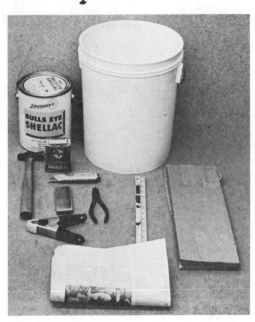

1. Hammer
2. Three or four ounce tacks
3. Razor knife
4. Diagonals or dykes
5. Pail
6. Cardboard
7. Spring clamp
8. Small block of wood
9. Stiff ruler — also used as a paper stuffer (optional)
10. Four or five pound cut white shellac
11. Old newspaper (optional)

PREPARATION

Clean the surface of the chair seat frame making certain that all dust, old nails, and tacks are removed. If there are any splits in the wood or defects in the rails, repair them before proceeding with the fiber rush weaving.

Fiber rush is an extremely strong material which will subsequently create a strong pull on the rails. Unlike cane and splint, the fiber rush itself needs no advance preparation. Prior to weaving, fiber rush should be placed in water for 15 to 20 seconds only to slightly soften the material. The fiber rush will have a tendency to disintegrate if it is thoroughly soaked or allowed to remain in the water too long. Also the fiber rush should be wound in a coil or any suitable method devised to allow ease in working and to keep the strands from becoming tangled or twisted.

Step # 1 Squaring

The weaving of square seats and the weaving of seats with longer front rails than back rails differs slightly. The shape that is not square will require the addition of extra pieces of fiber rush called "starters" to square off the design and obtain the necessary symmetry in the pattern weave. (There are

no "enders" in the case of fiber rush because the "starters" are the "enders.") To fill in with "starters" on the front of the chair seat, measure the length of the front and back rails and subtract the back rail length from the front rail length. Divide the remainder in half. Mark this distance with a pencil on the front rail from the corner posts, as pictured. Cut off enough fiber material, or about 3-1/2 times the length of the front rail, which will provide sufficient material to complete two lines of weave.

Dampen the rush fiber briefly in warm water. Fold the fiber material in half and tack it to the inside of the left side rail approximately two inches from the left front corner of the chair, as illustrated. Next take one end of the material and bring it over the front rail. Pull it hard to insure strong tension, but not strong enough to pull the tack away from the rail. Wrap the end around the front rail and bring it up over the previous fiber and the left rail as close to the corner as possible. It is most important to maintain the fiber rush at right angles with itself. Do not pull hard on the fiber but make certain it is secure to prevent lumping.

Follow this step by wrapping the fiber around the left rail, bringing

it along the adjoining front rail across to the rail on the right side. Now pull the fiber hard being very careful not  to break it. Next, move the fiber around the right rail going over the top first. Then bring the fiber up over the previously woven fiber and over the front rail on the right side as close as possible to the right front post or leg. From here it is wrapped around the front rail and tacked to the inside of the right rail near the front.

When the first fiber was tacked, an end remained which should now be used to repeat the same process over again. Continue to add starter pieces, weaving them until the seat has been squared off. Add three to four inches to every new starter  piece. This makes up for the added distance the fiber must move around the rails where it is to be tacked in place on the inside of the rails. The seat should now be squared off and the weaving process can begin.

Step #2 Weaving

As the weaving progresses, it is advisable to make accurate right angles since those that are not precise will tend to cause the entire pattern to grow gradually off balance. Therefore, it is suggested to pull fairly hard on the fiber when it is moving along the rails, but do not pull hard at the corner points. Use your thumb and forefinger to form right angles at the corner points. The hammer or mallet and wood block can be used to pound the fiber in place to attain accurate right angles. The pounding motion will compact the fiber and should be done against the rails. It will be helpful to pound a few fiber strands after they are woven rather than waiting until 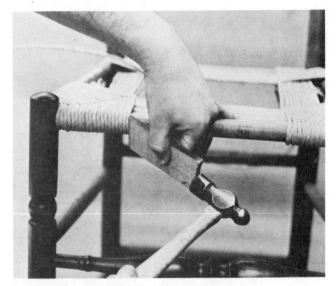 many strands have been woven, as the pounding will become more strenuous and less effective. Coil off sufficient fiber to fit comfortably in the hand for ease of control while working.

Tack the fiber rush onto the inside of Rail #1. Work the strand over and around Rail #2 at the same time pulling hard along Rail #1. Come upward with the fiber and make a right angle. Pass

See Diagram A p. 48

Correct Flow of Woven Fiber

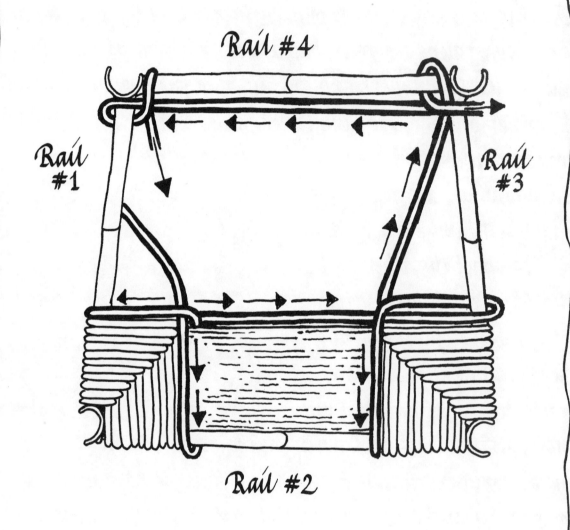

Rail #4

Rail #1

Rail #3

Rail #2

Diagram A

over the fiber and over Rail #1 and pull hard along Rail #2. Move over and around Rail #3 coming upward and into a right angle, weaving over and around Rail #2. Pull hard along Rail #3 moving over and around Rail #4. Come up and make a right angle. Passing over the fiber, weave over and around Rail #3. Pull hard along Rail #4 moving over and around Rail #1. Coming up to create a right angle, pass over the fiber and over and around Rail #4. Repeat the entire weaving process and continue until a new piece of fiber rush is to be added.

When coming to the end of the first piece of fiber rush, leave approximately six inches hanging over the rail. The rush should always end under and along one of the rails, in order to hide the knot that joins the new and old pieces of fiber. This will help to maintain neatness and uniformity in appearance.

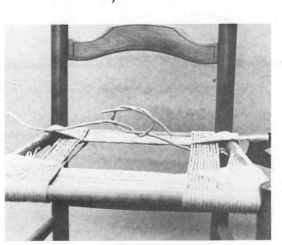

Wind enough of the fiber in the hand so it feels comfortable, dampen it and tie a square knot as in the picture. Cut off the excess fiber after the knot is tied. Continue to weave as before, remembering to hammer or pound the fiber periodically with the wood block or wedge to maintain the fiber at right angles with the rails.

Step #3 Stuffing

Insertion of cardboard into the seat structure gives it strength while maintaining the basic shape and improving the overall appearance. Therefore, when the weaving process extends to the point where approximately four inches of space remains on the side rails, cardboard cut in the actual seat shape can be inserted into the space between the top and bottom weaves. This should be done on the sides only as the front and back pieces of cardboard will be added at a later time. To insure that the

cardboard is cut in the correct shape, lay a piece on the top of the side rail and cut it into a triangle slightly smaller in area than the actual side of the chair seat. The points of the triangle are then inserted between the top and bottom layers of fiber material.

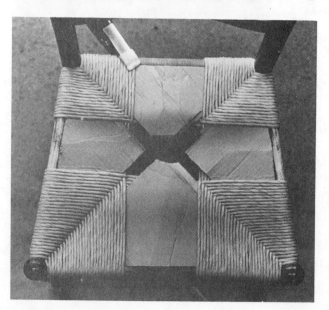

As each chair seat will differ, good judgment should be exerted in determining the bulk of the stuffing; it is imperative that the stuffing not become bunched or lumpy. Although it should remain solid and firm overall, too many layers of stuffing will, conversely, make the seat hard and uncomfortable for sitting. The next stuffing step will be described near the completion of the chair seat.

After the side cardboard is inserted, continue to weave in the manner described until approximately four inches remains unwoven on the front and back rails. Then place the cardboard stuffing pieces in the front and rear sections between the woven layers of fiber rush. On many chairs, the front and back rails are lower in position in relation to the side rails. If this is the case, an additional layer or two of cardboard stuffing can be placed in the front and rear sections only. Now, cut off all of the cardboard points that extend out into the middle of the seat. Continue to weave as before and at exact right angles. Once the weaving is completed on the side rails, space will remain on the front and back rails which must be filled in completely. This space, once it is filled, is referred to as the bridge of the fiber rush seat.

Step #4 Bridging

This basic weaving step is a "figure eight" pattern. To begin the bridge, bring the fiber rush upward through the center opening and weave it over Rail #2. Then weave around Rail #2 and bring the fiber up through the opening again. Move across the previously woven fiber and over and around

52

See
Diagram B
p. 53

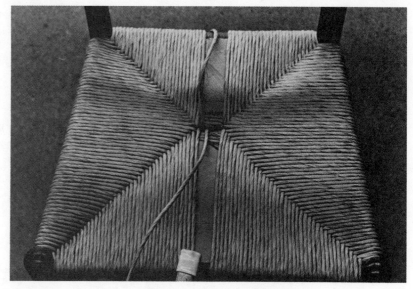

Rail #1. This same pattern is to be continued until the space on the front and back rails is completely filled in.

Step #5 Finishing

The end of the fiber rush should then be tacked onto the back rail on the underneath side and the excess cut off. If you choose to stuff your seat with paper, be extremely careful not to use too much in any one spot. Use a stiff wooden ruler to aid in the stuffing process. The only time a fiber rush seat warrants stuffing is when the lines on top of the seat are not "laying" flat. The stuffing will push the cardboard and the loosely woven fiber up, enabling all the woven lines of fiber to "lay" flat.

Now, rub the entire seat surface with the edge of the wooden block that you used for knocking the fiber into place along the rails. This is done to make certain that all lines lay flat and that any rough spots are smoothed down.

The final step is the shellacking of the seat. This is

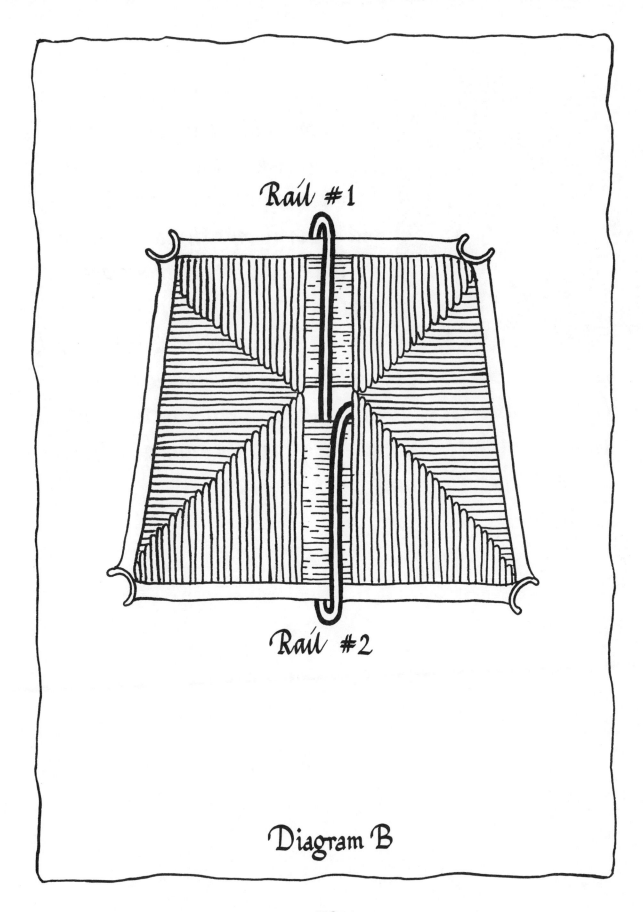

Rail #1

Rail #2

Diagram B

done to protect the fiber material from wear and should be done once a year to prolong the life of the seat. Take a small amount of shellac and brush it onto the seat. Either one thick coat or two thin coats may be used.

Fiber rush is the most durable material in the "caning family." It is impervious to an incredible amount of abuse, making it very practical for home decorating. The only thing that can damage a fiber rush seat after it has been woven is water.

Chapter 4
Splint

Splint, less common than cane or fiber rush, is used for the construction or replacement of chair seats. Splint is also a natural material cut from any one of a variety of hard woods such as hickory, ash or oak and can be purchased by the hank. The splint used in this chapter was cut from rattan. This is the most common splint material used today. The material lends itself to several woven designs usually associated with early American handcrafted furniture. The weaving pattern illustrated, called the herringbone design, was accomplished using a simple basic chair. Splint seats are comfortable and durable. Weaving with splint is suggested for the beginner, because the material is easily handled and the technique is relatively simple to perform.

TOOLS and MATERIALS

In addition to the chair frame and a supply of splint, the following tools are needed.
1. Hammer
2. Three or four ounce tacks
3. Stapler (ordinary house stapler is sufficient)

4. Spring clamp
5. Shears or tin snips
6. Razor knife
7. Ruler
8. Large blunt screwdriver
9. Rag or sponge
10. Very fine sandpaper
11. Pail for soaking splint

PREPARATION

The preliminary step is to make certain all of the chair rails are cleaned of old materials and staples. If the rails are damaged or broken, they are to be replaced prior to commencement of the weaving process. In addition, the splint is to be soaked in warm water for approximately 15 minutes, working with five or six pieces at a time. They are to be replaced in the water as they are used to maintain a ready supply of damp, pliable splint. All splint has a right and wrong side and this can be easily determined. When bending the splint in one direction or another, the right side will remain smooth in texture whereas the wrong side will scale and splinter. Of course, the smooth side should be worked to appear on the surface of the chair and the splintered side on the underside of the seat. Nevertheless, slight split lines can be detected in all splint, including the best quality, and these are a natural occurrence.

Step # 1 Wrapping

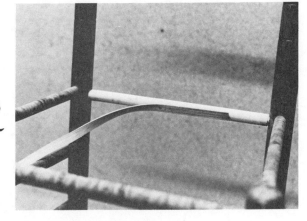

Begin by attaching the first strip of splint to the inside edge of the back rail with a tack, leaving four to five inches of splint overlapping, as illustrated. Then wrap the splint around both side rails moving back and forth. While the splint should remain firm, it should not be pulled tight as it will tighten when it dries. Upon completion of the first piece, allow for six to eight inches of overlap on the bottom of the seat, holding the piece in place with the spring clamp. The additional strips or pieces of splint are to be joined using three or four staples and insuring that the correct side of the splint has been established in advance and matched before stapling. Continue wrapping the rails and attaching additional pieces of splint, as needed, until

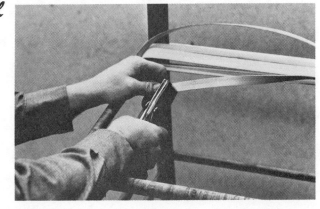

both side rails are covered. No uncovered spaces on the rails should remain when the wrapping has been completed. Tack the end of the final piece to the inside edge of the front rail allowing four to five inches of splint to overlap. Dampen the seat with water. This will keep it pliable for the weaving step.

Since the majority of chair seats are wider in the front than in the back, it will be necessary to insert additional pieces of splint called "starters" and "enders." Most chair seats require two "starters" and two or three "enders." To do this, measure the back rail and the front rail and subtract the back measurement from the front measurement. Divide the remainder in half. Measure this amount from the inside edge of the front rail and mark it with a pencil. Follow this same procedure on both sides. The marked spaces are to be filled in with "starters" and "enders" in order to square off the seat.

Step #2 Weaving

The herringbone pattern is woven in a very simple design. To accomplish this design requires weaving over three strands and under three strands and is the pattern used in this case. There are several standard variations on this design.

An individual may also create his own designs once he becomes familiar with the material and the basic weave. Begin by weaving over one strip and under three and continue by weaving over three and under three. Push the end of the "starter" down where it normally goes, as pictured. Allow the end to remain hanging until all of the "starters" are in the appropriate places.

The second "starter" begins by weaving over two and under three, etc. The next line follows by moving over three and under three. In order to maintain the herringbone design, after the first lines have been woven over one, over two and over three, the process is now reversed. The next, or fourth line, begins by weaving under one and over three, then under three and over three, etc. The next strip then goes under two, over three, under three, etc. and the following strip is woven under three, over three, in the same progression. The process again reverses by repeating the weave over one, under three, over three, etc. until the chair seat is completed in this manner. Next, take the starter closest to the side rail and weave it into the bottom of the seat. The seat should be woven in the same pattern on the top and bottom. Weave in all of the starters and continue them to the back rail if possible. This precludes the possibility of those strips becoming undone.

After the starters are in place, add a strand of splint on the bottom of the chair seat and weave this all of the way to the back rail. Turn the chair over and weave this piece in the top of the chair in the previously described manner.

To add new pieces of splint, make sure the piece of splint that you just finished weaving reaches to the front rail and ends there. Weave in a new strip of splint directly on top of the previous piece. Be certain it remains directly on top and fits snugly in place. This will keep both the old and new pieces from coming detached. Continue to weave until the back rail is completely covered remembering to dampen the splint when it appears dry or inflexible. As the weaving

nears completion, the splint may become more difficult to maneuver and the large blunt screwdriver can be utilized to provide assistance.

Once the back rail is completely filled in, all that

remains of the weaving process involves the "enders." This procedure is the same as for the "starters." The last piece of splint is woven on top as the last "ender." It is cut off and placed down in the appropriate position. Continue putting "enders" in until the entire front rail is filled.

Step #3 Finishing

All splint material has "hairy" residue on the surface. This can be removed with the fingers or a razor knife. Then the splint can be finely sanded to remove the very tiny "hairs" on the surface. The splint seat should be allowed to dry for at least 24 hours. If desired, after the seat has properly dried, stain can be added to simulate an aged appearance. If the splint is left

in its natural state, it will darken in color with age. As with the caned seats, the splint seat should be dampened with water once each month to retain its shape and durability.

Chapter 5
Weaving - Utilizing Six Millimeter Binding Cane

Six millimeter binding cane is another frequently utilized member of the "caning family." It comes from the same plant as hand and machine cane, however it is cut wider and thicker. Binding cane is available in widths of four, five and six millimeter. When working with these wider widths of cane, it is desirable to use first quality material which is uniform in color, width and thickness, as flaws are more easily noticed in the wider materials. Also, all knots should be shaven especially smooth.

All large width binding canes can be woven into many different designs that are both useful and attractive. The pattern design chosen for this particular chapter is easy to accomplish, making it an excellent project for the beginning craftsman.

TOOLS and MATERIALS

In addition to the footstool and a supply of six millimeter binding cane, the following tools are needed.

1. Hammer

2. Three or four ounce tacks
3. Razor knife
4. Diagonals
5. Pail
6. Spring clamp
7. Stapler and staples

PREPARATION

Before starting, make certain that all rails to be wrapped with the caning material are free from tacks, staples and any old caning material. In addition, if the rails are cracked or split, they are to be replaced before the actual weaving process begins.

Soak the cane material 15 minutes in warm water, remembering to soak three or four strands at a time and to replace each strand in the water as it is used. Check each piece of cane for cracks or large unsightly knots. If they appear, do not use that piece of cane as it will spoil the appearance of the finished product.

Step #1 Wrapping

Start by tacking the first strand of cane to the inside of one of the short rails. Be sure to leave a short length of cane material overlapping as pictured. The wrapping process proceeds

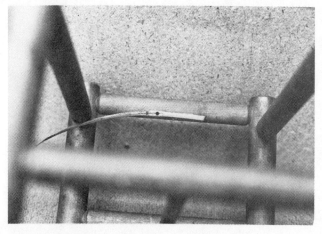

over the left rail. Continue to the right side rail and wrap around, bringing the cane across the bottom of the bench back to the left rail. Make another wrap around the two rails in the same manner as the first. Now go across to the right rail and put two wraps of cane around the right rail and secure with a spring clamp. Go across to the left rail and make two wraps around the left rail. Secure with a clamp, and continue the wrapping process.

To add a new piece of cane material, cut off the old piece, leaving five or six inches overlapping the rail. Overlap the old and new pieces of cane

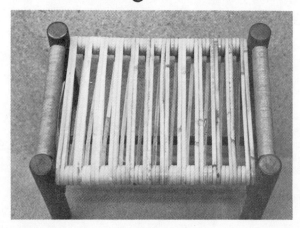

approximately three or four inches. Staple together using three or four staples. Continue to wrap as before, until the entire length of the rails is completely covered. Remember as you are wrapping to dampen the cane often to keep it moist and pliable. Ending off the last piece of cane is done in the same manner as the first piece was started. Tack to the inside of the remaining side rail, cut off and leave a three or four inch tail overlapping.

Step #2 Weaving

Turn the bench over and begin by weaving over two, under two, over two, under two, etc., until the first strand is woven all the way to the back rail. Make sure to push this line close to the side rail. This prevents it from getting in the way of the next woven line. Turn the bench right side up and begin by weaving over two, under two, over two, under two, etc., across the entire top of the bench, being careful to keep the line as straight as possible. Now turn the bench over and weave over and under the same lines that were woven over and under when the first piece was used. Turn to the top again, and

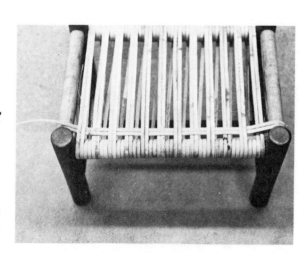

weave the next line in precisely the same manner as the first line. The next bottom line is woven exactly opposite to the first two lines; where they went over, this line goes under and where they went under, this line goes over. The next line on top is also woven opposite to the first two.

Adding a new piece of six millimeter cane material is done in exactly the same manner as adding a new piece of splint material. Weave the old piece of cane to the front rail, cut off any excess, and place a new piece of six millimeter cane on top of the old piece, weaving the entire way to the back rail. Continue weaving in this design of two over and two under until the entire bench is completed.

Step #3 Finishing

Because six millimeter cane is very large and coarse, it is not recommended that the caning material be stained. Rather, it can be painted or varnished after a 24 hour drying period has elapsed. The natural aging process will darken the cane, and give it an attractive patina. As with all natural cane material, six millimeter binding cane should be dampened once a month for long life and increased durability.

Chapter 6
Wicker

The construction of wicker furniture pieces will be described in two separate projects — a wicker plant stand and a wicker chair. In the previous chapters, the workshop projects primarily utilized preconstructed furniture and effected its repair or restoration, whereas the steps outlined for the wicker projects include the basic building of these items as well. Working with wicker differs from cane, fiber rush and splint as these materials and techniques utilize basic weaving skills while wickerwork is a plaiting technique. The results are distinctive because the warp elements are rigid rods, poles or stakes and the cross elements may be either stiff or flexible substances, usually rattan, as described herein. The articles produced are subsequently hard in texture and quite solid, durable and resistant to stress. Wicker furniture and artifacts have enjoyed popularity in past decades and, currently, there is a revival of interest displayed by manufacturers, decorators and consumers. Wicker materials and wickerwork techniques can be employed successfully and imaginatively in the creation of many other items including baskets, stools and trays. The only limit on the production of wicker furniture is one's own imagination.

Project I – Wicker Planter or Fern Stand

TOOLS and MATERIALS

1. One piece of 3/4 inch plywood, six inches wide and 16 inches long to be used for the base
2. Four rattan poles approximately 1–1/4 inches in diameter and 30 inches long for the legs
3. Two pieces of 5/8 inch rattan, 13–1/2 inches long to be used for braces
4. Two to three bunches of natural wicker or unshaven rattan (called pullet) 1/8 inch in diameter
5. Forty-one pieces of 3/16 inch size round reed used as stakes (supports)
6. Hammer
7. Pliers
8. Screwdriver
9. Drill with two bits, 3/16 inch drill bit and 1–1/8 inch flat drill bit
10. Rasp file
11. Hand saw or sabre saw

12 . Four 1-1/4 inch screws

13. Glue

14. One piece of five millimeter binding cane

15. Large container for water

CONSTRUCTION
Step #1 Base

1) Measure off 3/8 inch all around the base from the outside edge and make a pencil line around the entire frame.

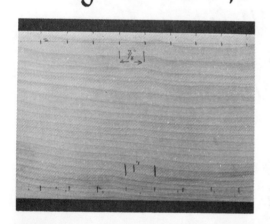

2) On one long side, measure off 7/8 inch across the entire side and make marks on the pencil line.

3) On the second long side, also measure off one inch segments and mark them, as pictured.

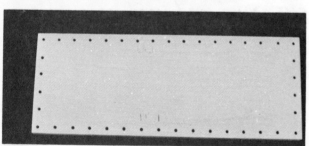

4) On two short sides, measure one inch segments and mark them off.

5) Drill 3/16 inch holes in all of the pencil marks indicated which will add up to a total of 41 holes drilled in the base.

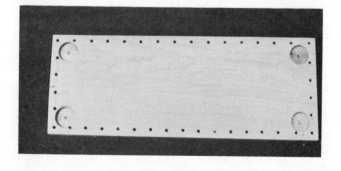

6) On the bottom of the base, measure one inch in and one

inch over and do this on all four corners.

7) Using the 1-1/8 inch flat drill bit, drill down 3/8 inch deep, but no deeper. Do this at all four corner points where your lines cross (see picture).

Step #2 Legs and Braces

1) On the four leg pieces, or rattan poles, measure off 3/8 inch from level and make a mark around the leg pieces.

2) With a rasp file, remove enough of the poles so that they fit tightly into the holes drilled on the bottom of the base.

3) Measure eight inches from the bottom of two of the legs or poles.

4) Mark these distances as they will indicate where the bottom braces will be attached.

5) Drill 5/8 inch holes at the marks on the two legs and make them 1/2 inch deep.

6) With the rasp file, remove enough of the surface on both ends of the short rattan pieces until the ends fit snugly into the holes in the leg pieces.

7) Repeat this same procedure using the other two legs and the remaining short rattan piece.

Then, put all of the legs and bracing parts aside as

they will be assembled after the top of the planter or fern stand is woven.

WEAVING

Step #1 Preparation

To begin, cut the forty-one upright pieces, or stakes.

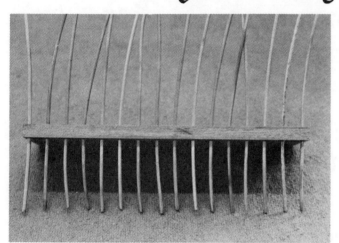

Place them into warm water for 15 or 20 minutes. When they are soaked and sufficiently pliable, insert them into the forty-one holes previously drilled into the base. Pull them through the holes with pliers pushing until four inches of the stake protrudes from the bottom of the hole. At this time, the natural pullet rattan is placed into the water to soak. Soak this material two hours to make absolutely sure it is completely saturated. Redampen the stakes.

Step #2 Braiding

Start at any corner moving in the direction of the left and bend and weave a rattan stake around two stakes and behind one, as shown, while making certain the stakes lie flat against the base form. Moving around the corners is done in the same manner and the procedure continues until the last three stakes remain unbraided.

Weave these into the bottom of the stakes that have already been woven and do this by moving over two and behind one just as was done with the others. (Wedge these in between the stakes already woven. Be as neat as possible.) This braiding holds the stakes in place and deters them from moving. At this point they should be dampened again as it is vital that the stakes remain damp and pliable to insure that they do not crack or split.

Step #3 Weaving the Pullet Rattan

Begin at any point on the top and start the weaving behind two stakes. This is done all around the top by moving the rattan in front of two stakes and weaving behind two stakes in a consistent pattern. It is most important to maintain straight stakes to establish uniformity and symmetry of the design and shape. It is also important to push or press each woven row down tightly on the top of every other woven row.

To add a new piece of pullet rattan, lay the new piece behind the stake on the left and continue until six

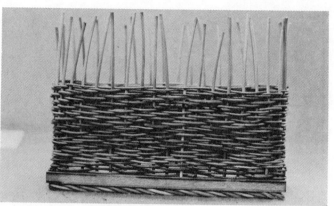

inches has been woven, as pictured. The stakes should remain damp and very straight during this process. To end off the stakes, the procedure is exactly as previously described in

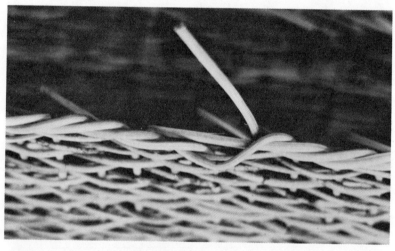

securing the bottoms of the stakes. That is by moving in front of two and behind one. Press down firmly. Continue until the entire top is completed with the exception of the last three stakes. Secure the last the stakes by joining as on the bottom. See photo for the proper procedure. Finish by cutting off all of the end pieces.

ASSEMBLING

Step #1

To join the legs and brace supports to the top piece, glue one cross piece support to two of the legs, forming a diagonal support. Glue the second cross support to the opposite two legs as shown.

Step #2

Attach the legs. To attach the first leg section, glue it, and place a 1-1/4 inch screw through the top of the base into each leg. Do this to the second leg section also. Where the supports cross, join them together with a piece of five millimeter binding cane weaving it in a figure eight design to insure strength.

FINISHING

Wicker can be most attractive if allowed to remain in its natural state. However, for decorative purposes, varnish or paint can be applied.

Project II ~ Wicker Chair

TOOLS and MATERIALS

1. Two pieces of 1-1/2 inch shaven rattan, 39 inches long
2. Four pieces of one inch shaven rattan, 13 inches long
3. Two pieces of 1-1/2 inch shaven rattan, 19 inches long
4. Ten to 15 pieces of six millimeter binding (first quality)
5. Two pieces of 3/4 inch rattan, 9-3/8 inches long
6. Two pieces of 3/4 inch shaven rattan, 13-1/4 inches long
7. Hammer
8. Nails ~ #6 head nails and #16, 1-1/2 inch finishing nails
9. Razor knife
10. Three or four ounce tacks
11. Stapler and 1/4 inch staples
12. Rasp file
13. Glue
14. Drill and 3/4 inch drill bit
15. Hand saw or sabre saw
16. Diagonals or dykes
17. Spring clamp

ASSEMBLY OF THE STRUCTURAL PARTS
Step #1 Legs and Rails

1) Cut two pieces of 1-1/2 inch shaven rattan 39 inches long which will form the back support of the chair and also the back legs.

2) Cut four pieces of one inch shaven rattan 13 inches long.

3) Cut two pieces of 1-1/2 inch shaven rattan 19 inches long which will be used for the front legs.

4) Bore two holes into each back upright piece. They are to be 3/4 inch holes drilled 18 inches from the ground.

5) Mark off 1/2 inch around each end of the four 13 inch rattan pieces, and chamfer off 1/4 inch or a sufficient amount to permit these to fit tightly into the holes previously bored.

6) Glue into place.

7) Repeat the same process on the opposite side.

8) After gluing the pieces, drive a nail in on either side using a #6 nail.

9) Take the front two legs and one chair rail and join them together with glue. Nail them securely in place.

10) Finally join the back section to the front section, as pictured.

Step #2 Bottom Bracing

1) As in the construction of the fern stand or planter, the bracing will be done diagonally.

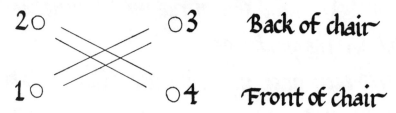

2○   ○3   Back of chair

1○   ○4   Front of chair

Numbers 1 and 3 are joined together
Numbers 2 and 4 are joined together

2) Cut two pieces of 3/4 inch rattan, 19 inches long.
3) Drill a 3/4 inch hole, 1/2 inch deep and six inches up from the floor on leg number 1 and leg number 3.

4) Drill the same size holes on legs number 2 and 4 except drill them seven inches from the floor.

5) Glue in first 3/4 inch rattan piece going from number 1 to number 3.

6) Glue in the second piece going from number 2 to number 4.

Step #3 Top and Back

1) Cut two pieces of 3/4 inch rattan, 13-1/4 inches long.

2) Drill two 3/4 inch holes, nine inches up from the back rail into the back uprights.

3) Drill two more 3/4 inch holes, 10 inches above the holes just drilled on the back uprights.

4) Glue the two pieces into place making certain to glue the bottom piece in first.

5) Nail these pieces into place using 1-1/2 inch, #16 finishing nails.

Step #4 Supports

The two supports are placed, as described, to hold the woven wicker back.

1) Measure in 3-1/2 inches from either side along the two back pieces just installed. Do this on both pieces.

2) Cut two pieces of 3/4 inch rattan, 9-3/8 inches long.

3) Install these two pieces at the 3-1/2 inch markings

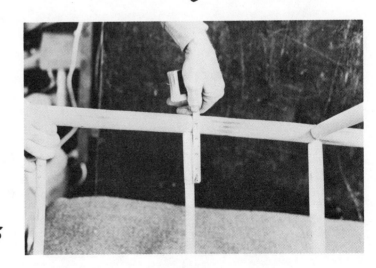

by using 1-1/2 inch, #16 finishing nails, noting that a pilot hole is not required since the rattan material is soft.

The basic substructure is now complete. The wicker seat and back are now ready to be woven into place. In addition, the legs and back uprights will be wrapped completely.

WRAPPING

The legs and back of the chair will be wrapped in six millimeter binding cane. Start by tacking the binding cane to the inside of one leg and wrap it up entirely. The tack

should be covered with the cane as the wrapping progresses. Use number three or number four tacks. Soak a few strands of the cane in water to insure its pliability and prevent breakage. As the wrapping continues, make certain each layer of cane is pushed up close to the next one that preceeded it. To end the pieces of cane, staple them into the inside of the back leg where they will not be

noticeable. To begin a new strand of cane, place the end of the new piece against the end of the former piece and staple it into place and continue wrapping as before. To wrap where the junction of the support and leg

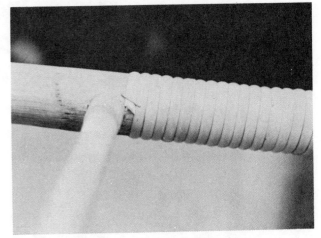

meet, staple the cane onto the support, wrap it around the leg and staple it to the other side. Cut off the excess ends of cane and continue the wrapping process until the entire area is covered.

For added strength, wrap around the staples that were just put in on the support member. Start by tacking as close to the inside of the leg as possible. Once the wrapping has covered all of the staples, continue to wrap two more

times. Then tack or staple the end to the underside of the support and cut off the end of the cane. Continue to wrap until reaching the next junction, or that of the side rail meeting

the front leg.

To wrap over the front upright, staple a strand of cane to the outside of the front leg. Wrap it over the top. Staple it to the top of the front rail. Cut off the cane. Continue until the entire top of the upright is covered. The next step is to wrap in the opposite direction around the same upright to completely cover the exposed staples. Continue

wrapping until all of the staples are covered; then wrap the cane around the cane ends that are stapled to the side and front rails. For added strength, wrap this in the same manner that the bottom support was wrapped. Wrap the other front leg in the same manner.

Wrapping the back legs is the same procedure as wrapping the front legs. The only exception is the junction of the side rail and the back upright of the chair. As on the front legs, staple strips of cane on the side rail and wrap them around the back upright. Staple onto the back rail and cut off the cane. The other leg is done in the same manner.

Next wrap the entire length of the back uprights

and do the junction points in the same manner as the previous junctions.

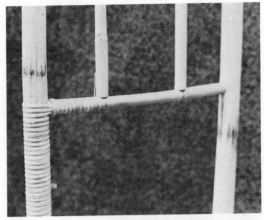

Areas A, B, C and D are to be wrapped.

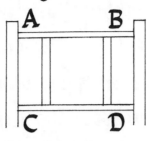

The tops of the back posts are wrapped in the same manner as the tops of the front posts with one exception. It is necessary to wrap around the two top knobs of the chair in a circle. Tack it in the back and end it in the back also. Cut off the ends of the cane. The wrapping is now completed and the weaving can commence.

WEAVING

Step #1 Preparation

The seat and back are woven of pullet rattan, the same material as was used in the fern stand, or planter. Begin by measuring the front and back rails and divide them into 12 equal sections. At each one

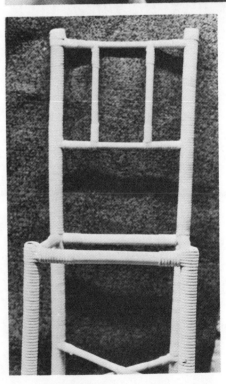

inch segment, put a pencil mark on both rails. This indicates where the "ribbing" or "warping" of the seat will be. The rattan is soaked in water before beginning the weaving process. The first step is to tack the rattan to the inside of the front rail. Wrap it around the rail and weave it across to the back rail, then around the back rail making sure to stay in line with the pencil marking on the rails. Tack the rattan to the inside of the back rail and cut it off. Now complete putting in the ribbing, as pictured.

Step #2 Wrapping

The next step is the wrapping of the rattan between the ribbing. The only wrapping that is not done is the four corners next to the rails. These are left unwrapped as there is insufficient space to accommodate the rattan which would have a tendency to distort the appearance of the chair. Start by tacking on the inside rail and wrap around the rail in between the ribs. To add another piece, tack and cut off the old piece and, then, tack and begin the new piece and continue the wrapping motion. The entire front and back rails are done this way with the exception of the corners next to the corner posts.

Step #3 Seat

The next step is the side to side weaving pattern and this begins at the left rear of the chair. Tack the rattan to the inside of the left rail and wrap it around. Now weave over one rib and under one rib, over one, under one, etc. across the entire seat. Wrap the rattan around the right rail and clamp it into place. Weave the rattan across the left rail going in the opposite direction moving under one, over one, under one, etc. to the back left rail wrapping it around this rail and weaving it back to the right rail. Continue, as before, wrapping it around the rail and clamping it. Then

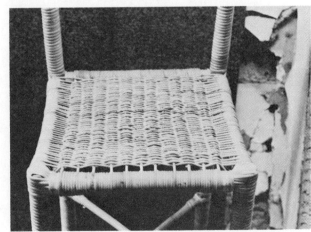

weave across, wrap around the back in the opposite direction, and clamp it.

To add new pieces, end the used piece by tacking it on the inside of the side rail. Tack the new piece in place and continue weaving. Proceed in the same manner until the entire seat is woven. Remember to alternate the lines of weave during this process. While weaving, it is important to dampen the rattan periodically and insure that the lines of weave are straight.

Step #4 Back

Weaving the back is done in almost the same manner as weaving the seat; however, there can be several variations of technique, one of which is described here. Measure off the distance on the top of the back and the bottom with four marks. In placing the ribs, tack the first ribs to the inside of the top piece. Leave a tail of rattan of 1/2 inch

 lying against the inside of the top rail. Bring the rattan down to the corresponding mark on the bottom and tack it in place. Also allow a 1/2 inch

tail of rattan against the inside rail and cut it off. The remainder of the ribs are now added. The tails are left intact so that they may be caught in the wrapping process. When

tacking the back, make sure to tack underneath the rail at all times so the tacks will not be visible. Wrap the back in the same manner

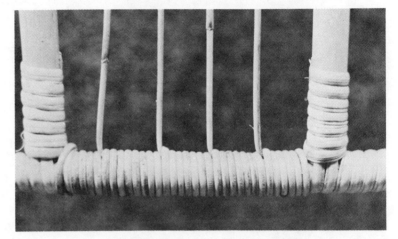

as the seat and be certain to wrap tightly over the tails, as pictured.

Weaving from side to side on the back is done in the same manner as the seat except, because there are so few ribs, it is necessary to pull the woven lines very gently and keep the ribs as moist and pliable as possible. When adding a new piece, end the old one by cutting it off and leaving two inches on the end. Put it in its correct place and let it hang

down. Weave the new piece toward the used piece, being careful to weave over and under the same ribs as the previously woven strand.

Place it next to the old piece and allow for approximately two inches excess remaining. The end pieces are cut off in finishing. Continue weaving until the entire back is completed.

FINISHING

The wicker can be left in its natural state or it may be painted or varnished to suit individual taste. Chairs of wicker are sturdy and comfortable as well as inexpensive to produce.

Chapter 7
Combination Wicker and Machine Cane Cocktail Table

This final project is unique because it affords the home craftsman a chance to combine the skills of machine caning and wickerwork. In order to achieve this interesting blend of a variety of textures, designs and shapes, superfine closewoven cane, 3/8 inch splint, round reed, 1-1/2 inch rattan poles and plywood are utilized. Each of the natural materials used retains its own special character, while joining together with the others to form this functional and decorative cocktail table.

TOOLS and MATERIALS

1. One piece of 3/4 inch plywood, 36 inches by 22-1/2 inches, used as the table top

2. One piece of 3/4 inch plywood, 30 inches by 16-1/2 inches, used as the bottom shelf

3. Four rattan poles, 1-1/2 inches in diameter and 18 inches long, used for the legs

4. Four blocks of 3/4 inch plywood, 3 inches by 3 inches,

     used for leg supports

5. One piece of 3/4 inch rattan, split in half lengthwise, as molding

6. Two pieces of superfine close woven machine cane — one piece 22 inches by 35 inches, and the other piece 16 inches by 29 inches

7. Three pieces of 3/16 inch tapered spline

8. One bunch of 3/8 inch splint

9. Sixty-three pieces of 3/16 inch size round reed, 10 inches long, as stakes

10. Hammer

11. Pliers

12. Razor knife

13. Wooden blocks for machine caning

14. Glue

15. Screwdriver

16. Drill with three bits — 3/16 inch drill bit, 1-1/2 inch flat drill bit, and 5/32 inch drill bit

17. Sabre saw

18. Router with 1/4 inch bit

19. Four, 2-1/2 inch, #10 screws

20. Sixteen, 1-1/4 inch, #6 screws

21. One counter sink

22. Natural plastic wood used to cover nails

23. 3/4 inch wire brads
24. Nail punch
25. One piece of extra fine sandpaper
26. Ruler
27. Awl

Step #1 Assembly of the Table Top

1) Take one piece of 3/4 inch plywood, 36 inches by 22-1/2 inches. This will be used as the table top.

2) On the bottom of this piece of plywood, mark a 1/2 inch border all around.

3) Along one long side measure off two inch increments and place these markings on the 1/2 inch border line.

4) Along the two short sides, also measure off two inch increments.

5) Along the final long side measure 1-1/2 inch increments and mark accordingly.

6) Now drill 3/16 inch holes, 1/2 inch deep — there should be sixty-three holes drilled.

7) Cut four pieces of 3/4 inch plywood, 3 inches by 3 inches. They will be used as leg supports.

8) At the four corners of the table top, on the underside, measure in 1-1/2 inches. Place a block down and trace around the block in pencil. Do this at all four corners.

9) Glue and screw the blocks into place. Use four, 1-1/4 inch, #6 screws in each block. Put one screw in every corner of each block.

10) Cut four leg pieces, 18 inches long from a 1-1/2 inch rattan pole.

11) Draw an "X" on each of the four blocks of wood by going diagonally from corner to corner. Where the lines cross is where the holes for the legs will be drilled.

12) Place the legs on the side, as they will be utilized later.

Step #2 Caning the Table Top

1) Route out a groove that is 1/4 inch wide by 3/16 inch deep.

2) Draw a line around the entire table top, one inch. This is where the groove will go.

3) Sand the groove, as in

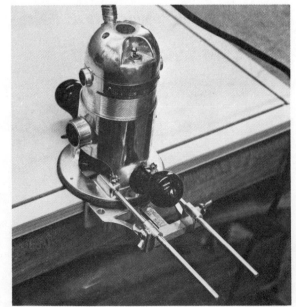

the machine caning section.

4) Take a piece of superfine closewoven cane, 22 inches wide and 35 inches long. Soak it in warm water 10 minutes.

5) Allow the cane to drain for two minutes before using.

6) When caning with superfine closewoven caning, be extremely careful to keep the cane as straight as possible.

7) Install the caning.

8) When removing the excess cane material, be very careful not to slip with the razor knife. The border of the table top has to remain scratch-free.

Step #3 The Wicker Work

1) Drill the four leg holes now. Take a 1-1/2 inch flat bit and drill the holes 5/8 inch deep at the "X" marks on the four blocks.

2) Cut sixty-three stakes out of 3/16 inch round reed, 10 inches long. Soak in warm water 15 minutes.

3) Dip one end of each stake into

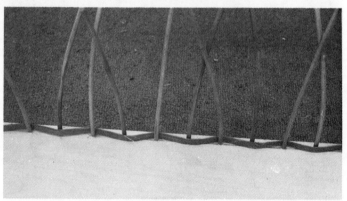

glue and then push each stake down until it hits the bottom.

4) Soak one bunch of 3/8 inch splint in warm water 15 minutes.

5) The weaving will go in front of one stake and behind one stake, around the entire length.

6) Adding new pieces of splint is done approximately in the same manner as adding new pieces to splint seat of a chair. The weaving has to be doubled behind one or two stakes.

7) Keep stakes damp as the work progresses.

8) Make sure each succeeding "layer" of splint is pushed down flush with the "layer" below.

9) Continue weaving until four inches of splint has been woven.

10) Braiding is done by going in front of one stake, and then behind the next stake.

11) Cut off the excess of the stakes after they have been woven.

12) Glue the legs into place.

Step #4 Putting the Bottom Shelf into Place

1) Take one piece of 3/4 inch plywood, 30 inches long and 16~1/2 inches wide, to be used as the shelf.

2) At the four corners of the shelf, on the underside, measure in 3/4 inch from both sides and make a mark.

3) Strike an arc equal to one quarter of a circle ~ the circle being the circle of the leg.

4) With a sabre saw, cut along the arc to create a notch. Do this to all four corners.

5) Route out a groove in the same manner that was used for the table top.

6) Cut a piece of cane 16 inches by 29 inches.

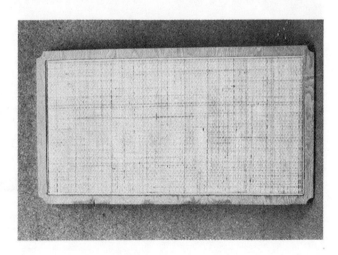

7) Apply the cane in the same manner as for the table top.

8) Measure up 12 inches from the top of the leg blocks along each leg, and mark each leg. This is where the bottom shelf will go.

9) Take a 5/32 inch drill bit and drill a hole through each leg, going on a diagonal line.

10) Before drilling, mark the spots where the holes are going to be drilled, with an awl.

11) Secure the shelf into place using four, 2-1/2 inch, # 10 screws.

12) Before securing the screws, countersink the holes drilled into the legs, so that the heads of the screws lie flat.

Step #5 The Molding

1) Take one, 3/4 inch rattan pole and cut it in half lengthwise.

2) Mitre all corners and apply the molding by using 3/4 inch wire brads.

3) Using a nail punch, tap the nail heads below the surface of the molding.

4) Fill with plastic wood.
5) Allow the plastic wood to dry.
6) Sand smooth.

Step #6 Finishing

This table can be left in its natural state or it can be stained or painted. However, before any finishing can be done, the plywood has to be sanded smooth using a very fine sandpaper. Any stain that is used will be absorbed readily by the plywood as well as by the cane and splint. It is recommended that a sealer, such as varnish, be used after staining. Paint should be applied with a sprayer, because a few light coats are better than one heavy coat. Also a paint primer should be applied to the exposed wood surfaces.

FINAL NOTE

As a final finishing "touch of class," a piece of plate glass can be placed on the top of the cocktail table. In order to do this, the only thing that should be changed in the construction of the table is the molding. Instead of using 3/4 inch rattan, use one inch rattan. Leave the additional 1/4 inch of the molding protruding above the top of the table. Have a piece of 1/4 inch thick plate glass cut to the exact size of the table, and place on the table top. It will lay completely flat with the top of the molding; and the molding will prevent the glass from sliding.

Summary

While the instructions provided will guide the craftsperson, it is hoped that the spirit of these special crafts will inspire the individual to further imaginative use of the materials. Mastering these techniques increases the knowledge and appreciation of fine furniture and artifacts, and particularly lends itself to experiencing the value of handmade objects. There is an undisputed feeling of pride and satisfaction in creating and using furniture and decorative items made with one's own hands.

Further, our intention is to suggest the variety of different designs and products which reflect the many ways the materials can be used. These diversified photographs will provide additional enlightenment to illustrate ways in which these crafts have enriched our environment and stimulated our interest.

Illustrations

Rocker — caned in 6 millimeter binding cane, done in herringbone design

Bench — done in 6 millimeter
binding cane, woven into unusual pattern

Splint armchair ~ seat and back

Hand caned bentwood settee converted to machine cane

Hand caned chair converted to
machine cane

Modern weave machine cane chair

Machine caned seat in Cesca chair

Machine cane bentwood side chair

Turn-of-the-century machine
caned baby's combination
high chair and stroller

Prague chair converted hand to
machine caning

Two fiber rush seats

Modern design hand caning

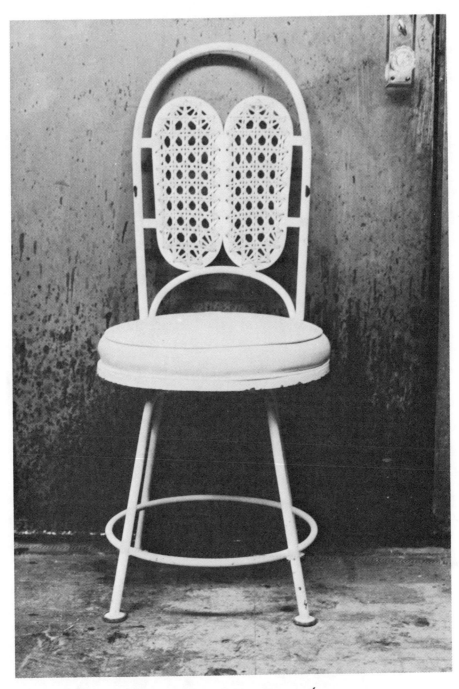

Open weave hand caning

Hand cane rocker seat and back

Restored hand cane antique arm chair

Baby rocker machine caned seat
and back

Box design fiber rush seat

Caned planter

Sources
For Caning Supplies

Veteran's Caning Shop, Inc.
550 West 35 Street
New York, N.Y. 10001   212~868~3244

ELI Caning Shop
86 Wood Road
Centereach, N.Y. 11720   516~585~0522

For Rattan Supplies

Peerless Rattan and Reed
   Manufacturing Company, Inc.
97 Washington Street
New York, N.Y. 10006

About the Author

John Bausert has been involved with handicrafts all of his life, learning the methods and techniques described when he was a young child. Now, an expert craftsman himself, John teaches his skills to others and supervises his experienced staff at the Veterans Caning Shop on West 35th Street in Manhattan. The family business, which he manages, began on East 56th Street almost seventy years ago and employs three generations of craftsmen. The shop  specializes in all types of hand caning, machine caning, natural and fiber rush and splint seating. His clientele includes large furniture manufacturers as well as individual customers. The shop is one of the few locations where supplies for these handicrafts can be purchased either in person or by mail order.